SCHOLASTIC

ACTIVE™ Grammar

Practice Book 2

Rosemary Allen

Name ______________________________

Class ______________________________

Previously published as Grammar Skills 2 by Learners Publishing Pte Ltd.

First edition 2012
Reprinted 2012, 2013 (thrice), 2014 (thrice), 2015 (twice), 2016, 2017, 2018, 2020, 2022, 2024, 2025, 2026

ISBN 978-81-8477-747-5

CONTENTS

 ISBN 978-81-8477-747-5

To Teachers and Parents

The study of English grammar in schools is changing as educators become increasingly aware of the important role context plays in language learning. The functional use of grammar has become a feature of English syllabuses around the world.

Active Grammar Practice Books have been written specifically to provide students with valuable links between basic, traditional grammatical concepts and the functional contexts in which they are used. The activities represent a blend of traditional and functional approaches to describe how texts 'work' in real-life situations and why certain grammatical choices are considered appropriate. Traditional grammar serves to provide students with the special terminology needed to talk about grammar, while functional grammar is intended to improve communicative competence by showing students how grammar works in the context of different text types.

The exercises in this book give students systematic guidance in developing an understanding of grammatical concepts. Throughout the books there are panel notes that give hints for correct usage and highlight exceptions to grammar rules, as well as provide simple non-technical definitions to help students understand the exercises. Many of the exercises incorporate learner-centred activities that include completing rhymes and short stories, solving riddles and puzzles, doing word searches and seeing 'language-in-action'. At the same time, the activities provide teachers with a range of techniques to use, techniques that have proven highly successful with both native and non-native speakers of English. The exercises are graded, but include challenging ones to motivate as well as interest the students.

It is hoped that teachers will find this series a valuable tool in their teaching programme, one that will provide young learners with a fascinating journey into the world of English language and a sound knowledge of how it works.

 ISBN 978-81-8477-747-5

1 The Alphabet

A ***This funny clown has forgotten some of the letters of the alphabet. Can you help him fill in the missing letters?***

Now fill in a, e, i, o and u to finish this sentence.

Th___s cl___wn c___n j___ggl___ tw___nty-s___x b___lls.

Did You Know

The letters **a**, **e**, **i**, **o** and **u** have a special name. They are called **vowels**. The other letters in the English alphabet are called **consonants**.

 ISBN 978-81-8477-747-5

B ***Each of these words has two vowels missing. Look at the picture clues and fill in the missing vowels.***

1. b___ck___t 
2. p___zz___ 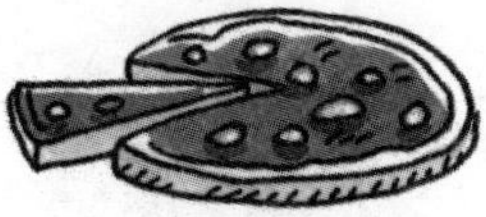
3. j___ ___p 
4. s___ ___l 
5. sch___ ___l 
6. m___ ___l 
7. b___ ___k 
8. c___b___ 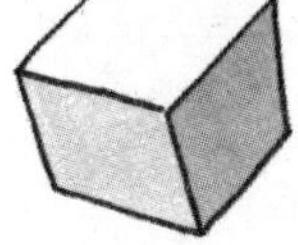
9. c___k___ 
10. b___ ___ns 

C ***Write two more words that have the same vowels as the given word in each box. The first one has been done for you.***

cake	moon	kite	beak
face	______	______	______
plate	______	______	______
tree	**sail**	**goat**	**loud**
______	______	______	______
______	______	______	______

 ISBN 978-81-8477-747-5

D *Some students are helping Miss Lee in the library. These are their names. Arrange them in alphabetical order.*

Siti Zena Eric

Grace May John Kate

Fuad Richard Dora

1. ____________ 6. ____________
2. ____________ 7. ____________
3. ____________ 8. ____________
4. ____________ 9. ____________
5. ____________ 10. ____________

Sort these book titles into alphabetical order for the library helpers.

1. ____________ 5. ____________
2. ____________ 6. ____________
3. ____________ 7. ____________
4. ____________ 8. ____________

 ISBN 978-81-8477-747-5

E Complete the four charts.

Fruit

a - apple

b - ______________________

g - ______________________

m - ______________________

p - ______________________

Vegetables

b - beans

c - ______________________

l - ______________________

p - ______________________

t - ______________________

Transport

c - cart

a - ______________________

b - ______________________

t - ______________________

v - ______________________

Sports

n - netball

b - ______________________

f - ______________________

h - ______________________

s - ______________________

 ISBN 978-81-8477-747-5

2 Determiners

A *Solve the riddles. You will find the answers in the box below.*

What am I?

1. I am an animal.
   I live in water.
   I look like a snake.
   I'm very slippery.

   I am ______________________

2. I am a fruit.
   I can be green, red or yellow.
   I grow on a tree.
   Some people say I keep the doctor away.

   I am ______________________

3. I am something you wear.
   I am made of leather.
   I have a buckle.
   I am worn around the waist.

   I am ______________________

4. I am an animal.
   I swim fast.
   I live in water.
   I have fins and scales.

   I am ______________________

5. I am something you wear.
   I can keep you warm.
   I can be made from wool.
   I am worn around your neck.

   I am ______________________

Select your answers from here.

an apron	a shoe	an eel	a mango	a tortoise
an apple	a crab	an orange	a fish	an overcoat
a glove	a belt	a shark	a scarf	a banana

 ISBN 978-81-8477-747-5

B Penny is in Mr Han's pet shop. Complete their conversation with *a*, *an* or *the*.

Penny : I want to buy (1) ________ cat, please.

Mr Han : Do you want (2) ________ young kitten or (3) ________ older kitten?

Penny : I want (4) ________ orange-coloured kitten.

Mr Han : (5) ________ orange kitten in this cage is sold. (6) ________ old man bought it.

Penny : Then, can I have (7) ________ black one in (8) ________ cage over there?

Mr Han : Certainly, you've made (9) ________ very good choice. He's (10) ________ active kitten.

Did You Know

The, **an** and **a** are called **articles**.

C Read the conversation again and find the words that follow *a*, *an* or *the*. List them in the correct box.

a ...	an ...	the ...
cat	older kitten	orange-coloured kitten

Write *a* and *an* to complete these rules:

1. We use ________ before nouns and words that begin with vowels.
2. We use ________ before nouns and words that begin with consonants.

Remember

You use **the** before a noun when people know which thing or person you mean.

 ISBN 978-81-8477-747-5

D Write *a*, *an* or *the* in the blanks to complete the sentences.

> **Did You Know**
>
> **The** is also used for special names like **the** Indian Ocean, **the** Singapore River.

1. ________ ant is ________ insect.
2. ________ bear is ________ large animal that lives in ________ cave.
3. There's somebody at ________ door.
4. He is wearing ________ old pair of shoes.
5. Susan borrowed ________ book from ________ library.
6. John missed ________ bus, so he took ________ taxi.
7. Mother bought ________ eggplant, ________ box of chocolates and ________ kilo of grapes from ________ supermarket.
8. There is ________ old church in ________ town of Hamelin.
9. ________ Amazon River is ________ longest river in South America.
10. Do you know ________ name of ________ tallest building in ________ world?

E Read these two sentences and look at the words in bold.

1. The little elephant walked a long way until he came to **a** river.
2. The little elephant walked a long way until he came to **the** Amazon River.

Why is* a *used in the first sentence and* the *in the second one? Write your reason here.

____

____

____

 ISBN 978-81-8477-747-5

F *Read the story. Underline the words **few, some, many, much** and **any**.*

ack was sitting in a park looking very ınhappy. There were not many people in :he park. An old man sat down next to him ınd asked Jack why he was so sad.

'I want to see a movie, but I don't have ıny money. My mum says that she loesn't have very much money to spare."

'When I was young," said the old man, "we lidn't have much money either. We had few :reats. My friends made some money by vashing cars, so that we could all go to the novies together. I guess very few people ;hare what they have these days."

'Maybe I could ask some neighbours if I :ould help them wash their cars. Then I night have enough money to take omeone to the movies with me. Would ou like to come?" asked Jack.

Did You Know

Special adjectives like **few**, **some**, **many**, **much** or **any** are called **determiners**. You can use these determiners to talk about amounts.

G *The words you have underlined are determiners that describe how much or how many. Write all the nouns that they describe in the story.*

)eterminers	Nouns
. few	treats, people
:. some	
3. many	
-. much	
:. any	

 ISBN 978-81-8477-747-5

3 Common Nouns

A *This map of a zoo shows you where you can see the animals. On the signboards, write the names of the animals. Use the words on the next page to help you.*

B *The words for young animals are also nouns. Write the missing nouns in these eight sentences.*

1. A ____________ is a baby hen.
2. A ____________ is a baby cat.
3. A ____________ is a baby cow.
4. A ____________ is a baby frog.

 ISBN 978-81-8477-747-5

polar bear	monkey	lion	hippo
orang-utan	ostrich	penguin	goat
	crocodile	sea lion	

Did You Know

Names of animals are **nouns**.

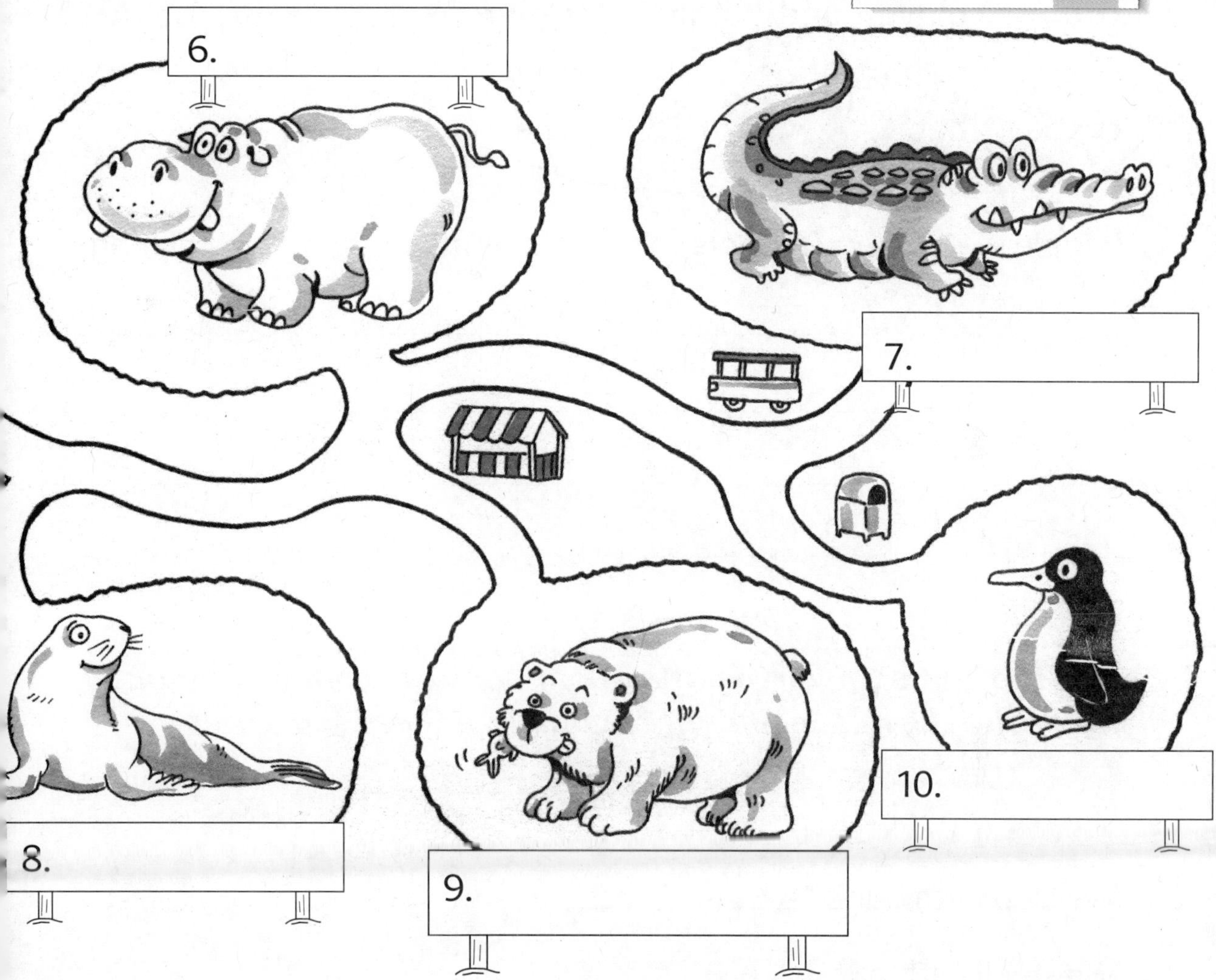

5. A ____________ is a baby dog.
6. A ____________ is a baby horse.
7. A ____________ is a baby duck.
8. A ____________ is a baby goat.

 ISBN 978-81-8477-747-5

C *Arrange these words in the correct group.*

dentist	calf	school	soap
cat	playground	pan	clown
frog	airport	car	king
castle	net	artist	ape

Did You Know

Words for things, animals, people and places are called **nouns**. All the nouns in the four lists are called **common nouns**.

People	Animals	Places	Things
________	________	________	________
________	________	________	________
________	________	________	________
________	________	________	________

D *The names given to parts of our body are common nouns. Write the missing nouns to complete these sentences.*

1. We see with our ________________.
2. We clap with our ________________.
3. We smell with our ________________.
4. We hear with our ________________.
5. We smile with our ________________.
6. We lick with our ________________.
7. We bite with our ________________.
8. We nod with our ________________.

 ISBN 978-81-8477-747-5

E *Complete the word puzzle by writing in the common nouns. Use the picture clues to help you.*

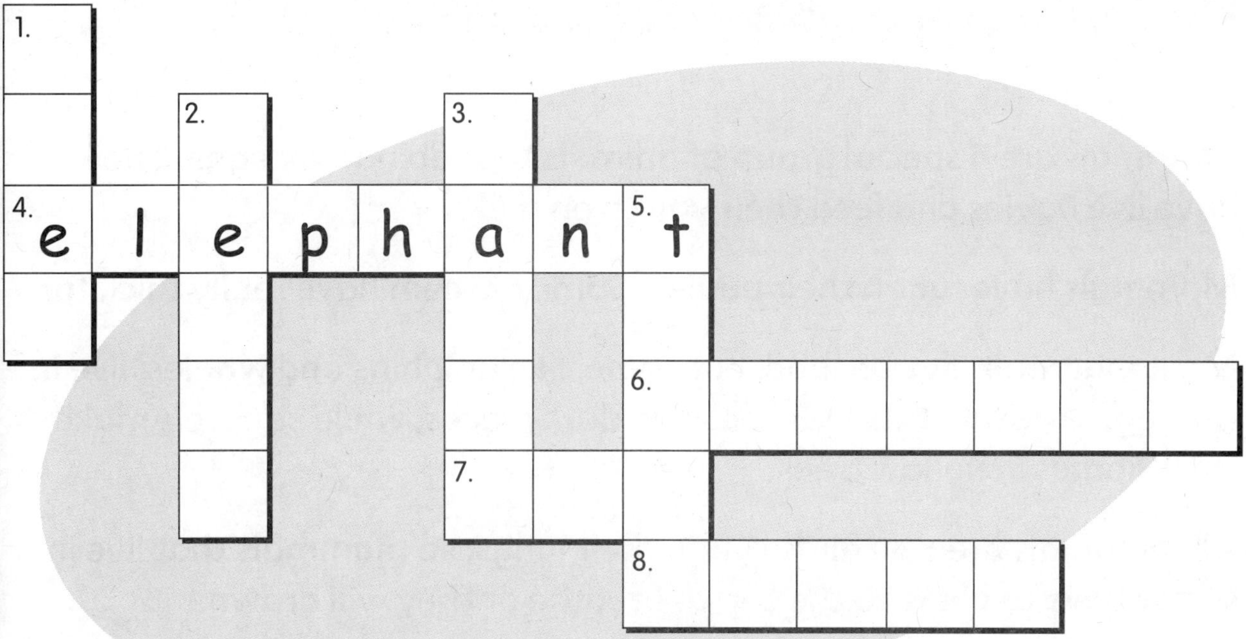

Picture clues

 ISBN 978-81-8477-747-5

4 Singular and Plural Nouns

A *Read this report about mammals.*
Then underline all the words for animals.

Mammals are a special group of animals that do not lay eggs. They have live babies and feed their young on milk.

Mammals have fur on their bodies. Some of them have really thick fur.

Most mammals live on land, but some, like dolphins and whales, live in the sea. Mice and rats build nests in dark places, while squirrels make their homes in hollow trees.

All mammals breathe air through their lungs, so mammals that live in water have to come to the top to breathe or they will drown.

Some mammals you may know are:

- dogs and cats
- goats and donkeys
- cows and oxen
- foxes and wolves

 ISBN 978-81-8477-747-5

B *Did you notice that the words you have underlined on page 16 are all plural nouns? List 8 of them in the left column. Then write their singular form in the right column.*

Plural nouns	Singular nouns
1. ________	1. ________
2. ________	2. ________
3. ________	3. ________
4. ________	4. ________
5. ________	5. ________
6. ________	6. ________
7. ________	7. ________
8. ________	8. ________

Did You Know

When you talk about one thing, it is **singular**. When you talk about more than one thing, it is **plural**. Common nouns can be singular or plural.

C *Do you add **-s** or **-es** to make these singular nouns plural?*

1. one **girl** two ________.
2. one **witch** some ________.
3. one **monkey** many ________.
4. one **baby** two ________.
5. one **pen** ten ________.
6. one **box** few ________.
7. one **pony** two ________.
8. one **boy** many ________.
9. one **banana** some ________.
10. one **dish** many ________.

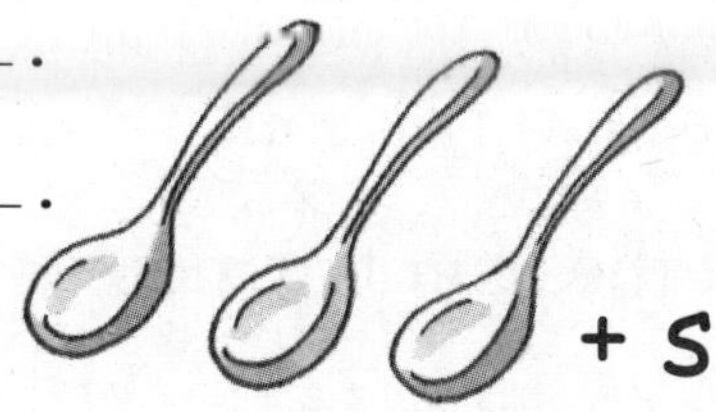

 ISBN 978-81-8477-747-5

D *The plurals of these singular nouns don't end in -s or -es. Do you know what their plurals are?*

1. child ______________________
2. deer ______________________
3. goose ______________________
4. sheep ______________________
5. woman ______________________
6. fish ______________________
7. tooth ______________________
8. reindeer ______________________

Did You Know?

Some plural nouns are **the same** as their singular form. But some are **different** from the singular nouns.

E *Complete the sentences with plural nouns.*

1. The plural of **house** is ______________________,
   but the plural of **mouse** is ______________________.

2. The plural of **fox** is ______________________,
   but the plural of **ox** is ______________________.
3. The plural of **pan** is ______________________,
   but the plural of **man** is ______________________.

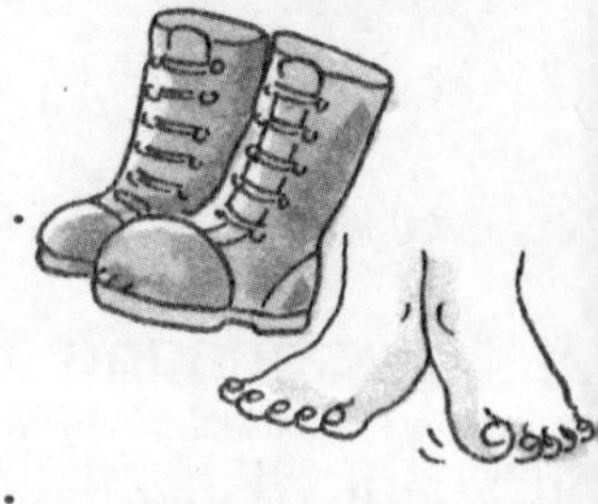

4. The plural of **boot** is ______________________,
   but the plural of **foot** is ______________________.

 ISBN 978-81-8477-747-5

5 Countable and Uncountable Nouns

A ***The picture shows different kinds of food that we eat every day to keep us healthy.***

1. Underline the food items that are plural. They are food items that can be counted.
2. Circle the food items that cannot be counted.

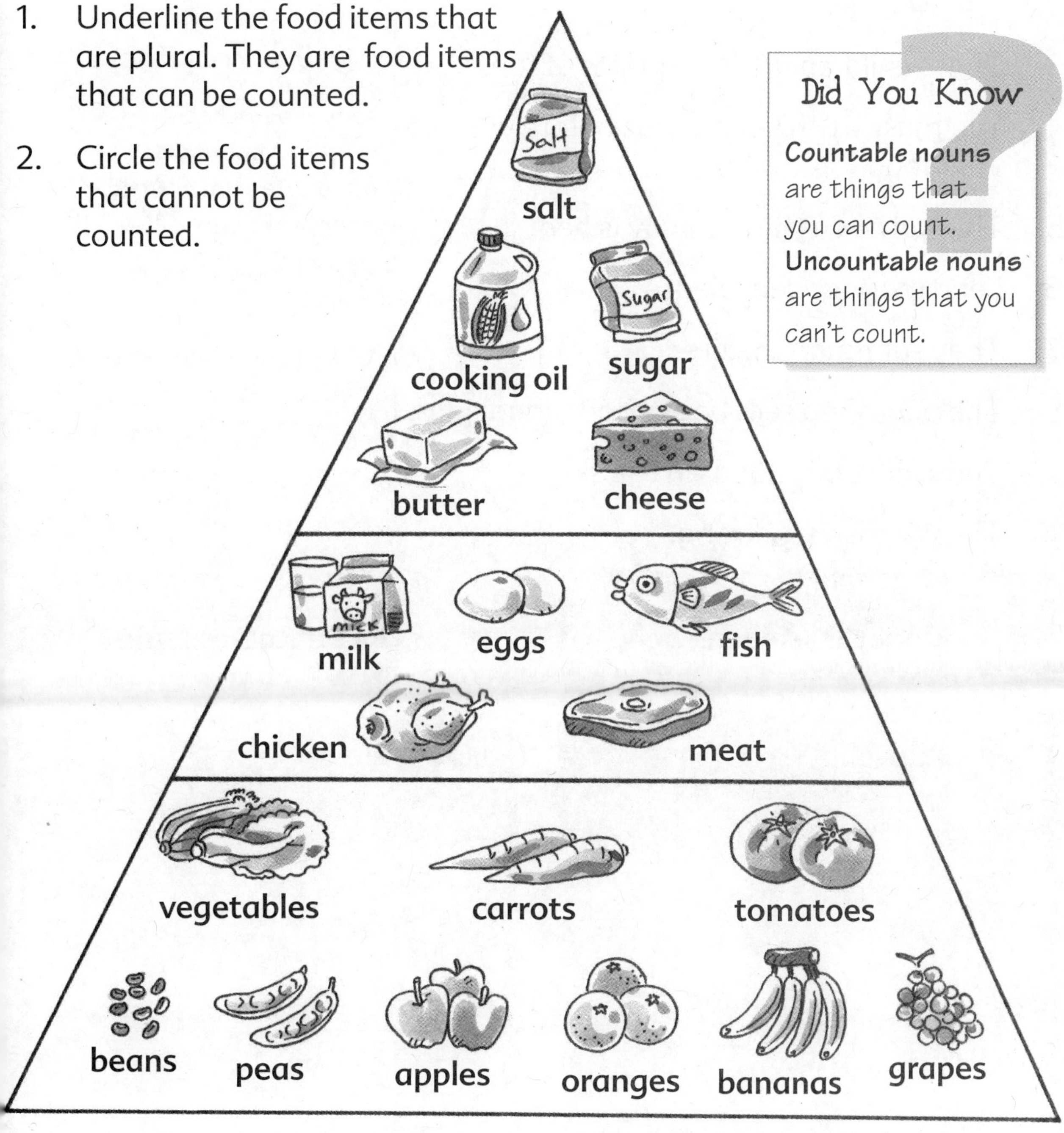

Did You Know?

Countable nouns are things that you can count.
Uncountable nouns are things that you can't count.

 ISBN 978-81-8477-747-5

B

Underline all the nouns in the sentences.
Which ones are countable nouns and which ones are uncountable nouns? Write your answers in the correct box below.

1. My sister hates cockroaches.
2. The weather is fine.
3. These children are having lots of fun.
4. You must wash your hands before you eat your food.
5. The traffic on the highway is heavy.
6. Lend me your pen, please.
7. They sat round the fire.
8. The bookshop sells books and magazines.
9. There are dark clouds in the sky.
10. The wind is very strong.

Did You Know?

To find out whether a word is a **countable noun** or an **uncountable noun**, ask yourself:

- Can I make the noun plural?
- Can I put a number in front of it?
- Can I put **a** before it?

Countable Nouns	Uncountable Nouns

 ISBN 978-81-8477-747-5

C *Look at the breakfast table. Colour the things that are* ***countable nouns*** *red and those that are* ***uncountable nouns*** *blue.*

D *Fill in the blanks with countable or uncountable nouns from the picture above.*

1. a few ______________________
2. a little ______________________
3. plenty of ______________________
4. some ______________________
5. an ______________________
6. four ______________________

Did You Know?

You can add a number or these words to countable nouns: **a, an, many, a few, lots of, some** or **any**.

You can add these words before uncountable nouns: **much, a little, some, any, plenty of** or **a lot of**.

 ISBN 978-81-8477-747-5

6 Masculine and Feminine Nouns

A *Read Paul's diary. Underline all the words for people.*

Tuesday, 9 December

At Christmas-time, my family and I went to London.

London is a big city in England. When we arrived, the first thing we did was to visit Buckingham Palace. I wish I could take a photo of Queen Elizabeth or Prince Charles.

The tour guide and the bus driver both told me that there are many important people in England, like lords and ladies, dukes and duchesses, but they don't all live in palaces.

Tomorrow we are going to the London Zoo.

 ISBN 978-81-8477-747-5

B ***Write the words you have underlined on page 22 in the correct lists. Add two more gender words of your own to each list.***

Masculine Nouns	Feminine Nouns	Common-gender Nouns

Did You Know?

Masculine nouns are words for males. **Feminine nouns** are words for females. **Common-gender nouns** are used for males or females.

 ISBN 978-81-8477-747-5

C Read the second page in Paul's diary.

Wednesday, 10 December

Today Aunt Mary took us to the London Zoo. It was fun, but it is not as big as the Singapore Zoo.

The usual animals were there — lions and lionesses, tigers and tigresses, bull elephants and cow elephants.

I also saw some animals I hadn't seen before like foxes, geese and peacocks. The fox was looking very proud because his vixen had four pups. The gander was very fierce when anyone went near the goose because they had seven little goslings. The peacock and peahen stayed very close to their chicks.

We had a good time at the zoo.

1. Match the masculine and feminine nouns.

uncle •	• niece
rooster •	• bride
stallion •	• hen
drake •	• aunt
groom •	• duck
nephew •	• mare

2. Write the feminine nouns.

lion ____________

tiger ____________

bull elephant ____________

fox ____________

gander ____________

peacock ____________

3. Think of an animal that is the father of these baby animals.

cub ____________

calf ____________

pup ____________

 ISBN 978-81-8477-747-5

D *Write the nouns in bold print in the correct box.*

	Masculine Nouns	Feminine Nouns	Common-gender Nouns
1. The **steward** is serving drinks to the **passengers**.	____________	____________	____________
2. The **maid** is mopping the floor.	____________	____________	____________
3. The **teachers** are in the staff room.	____________	____________	____________
4. **Mum** bought a T-shirt for my **cousin**.	____________	____________	____________
5. A lot of **people** take a walk in the park in the evening.	____________	____________	____________
6. The **children** are flying kites on the beach.	____________	____________	____________
7. The cinema is showing the **Lion** King.	____________	____________	____________
8. **Tim** bought a CD-ROM.	____________	____________	____________
9. The **zookeeper** is feeding the animals.	____________	____________	____________
10. The **duke** bowed to the **queen**.	____________	____________	____________

 ISBN 978-81-8477-747-5

7 Proper Nouns

A *Read about Maggie's visit to London. Underline all the proper nouns.*

During the school holidays, Maggie and her parents flew to London with Singapore Airlines They left Singapore on 10 June.

They stayed at the Regency Hotel. They went to the Tower of London, the British Museum and Hyde Park. They also went to the famous Harrods department store to buy some souvenirs for Maggie's friends, Nancy, Doris and Ben. Maggie also bought a photo frame for her Uncle Andy and Aunt Susie.

Maggie enjoyed her holiday.

B *Find the proper nouns for **people** or **places**. Write them in the correct box.*

People	Places
Maggie	London

Remember

Proper nouns begin with capital letters.

 ISBN 978-81-8477-747-5

C ***Rewrite these sentences using capital letters for the proper nouns.***

Did You Know

Only the important words in book titles or movies need to have capital letters.

1. mary, john and david were helping miss lee, the librarian, in the school library. Their school is in chestnut road.

2. john took four books to the children's section. They were alice in wonderland, aesop's fables, harry potter and gulliver's travels.

3. mary took three books to the reference section. They were first learners' dictionary, english for children and the world atlas.

4. david took two books to the history section. They were a history of the world and famous battles.

5. miss lee thanked the children for helping.

 ISBN 978-81-8477-747-5

D Write the proper nouns using correct capital letters.

1. Write the names of two movies you have enjoyed.

2. Write the names of your two favourite books.

3. Write the names of two of your friends.

4. Write the names of four rivers.

5. Name a place where you would like to go for a holiday.

6. List three special holidays celebrated in your country.

 ISBN 978-81-8477-747-5

E Complete the story by adding proper nouns.

Today was ______________________ (a day of the week), so Tom didn't have to go to school.

He was bored, so he rang his friend

______________________ (name of a boy) who lived in

______________________ (name of a street or place).

"Let's go to ______________________ (name of a cinema),

I want to see the movie ______________________ (name of a movie)."

"I'd rather see ______________________ (name of a movie)," said his friend.

"I've already seen that," said Tom, "so let's do something else."

"We could go for a swim at ______________________ (name of a swimming pool or beach)," suggested his friend.

"Let's go shopping instead at ______________________ (name of a department store)," replied Tom.

"OK, I'll meet you at ______________________ (name of a place, a bus or train station) at half past ten and then we'll decide."

"Goodbye. See you later," said Tom and hung up.

 ISBN 978-81-8477-747-5

8 Pronouns

A *Use these pronouns to complete Peter's description of his family. You may use some pronouns more than once.*

Hello, my name is Peter. ________ live in the city with my mother and father and two sisters. My father is a teacher. ________ works very long hours. My mother is a lawyer, but ________ only works part-time. My sisters and ________ try to help our parents as much as ________ can. My sisters help in the kitchen. ________ wash and dry the dishes. ________ make my own bed and keep my room tidy. ________ have a cat called Ginger. ________ has lived with ________ for a long time.

B *Look at the pronouns at the top of this page again. Some of them refer to only one person. Others refer to more than one person. Sort them into singular and plural pronouns.*

Singular Pronouns	Plural Pronouns
I	we
________	________
________	________
________	________

Did You Know

Pronouns are words that can be used instead of common nouns or proper nouns.

 ISBN 978-81-8477-747-5

C Add a pronoun to complete the sentences.

1. The bird sat on a branch. ________ had a worm in its beak.
2. John was not happy. ________ had a bad cold.
3. Peter and Sue were excited. ________ were going to the circus.
4. My marks are not good. ________ did not study very hard.
5. Linda is a good student. ________ does her homework.
6. John, do ________ play the guitar?
7. My brother and I play football. ________ play in the school team.

D Add a suitable pronoun to complete the sentences.

1. Linda is my friend. She sits next to ________ on the bus.
2. Peter's shirt was a mess. He had torn ________ .
3. John and Sue wrote from London. The postcard was for all of ________ .
4. I don't have a favourite subject at school. I like ________ all.
5. Amy, my sister, asked me to return this book to ________ .
6. My mother is feeling better. The doctor has moved ________ to a different ward.
7. It was Dad's birthday on Tuesday. We gave ________ a new watch.

 ISBN 978-81-8477-747-5

E Add a suitable pronoun in the second sentence.

1. The children are camping.

   ________ are pitching a tent.

2. My name is Mike.

   ________ am eight years old.

3. Janet is using the phone.

   ________ is talking to her friend.

4. The dog is fierce.

   ________ is barking at the stranger.

5. This model plane is made by Peter.

   ________ has made it by himself.

6. Peter and I study in the same school.

   ________ are good friends.

7. John, you are late again.

   ________ have missed the bus.

8. Girls, our team has won.

   ________ have done well!

F Re-write the second sentence using short forms.

1. They're pitching a tent.
2. ________________________________
3. ________________________________
4. ________________________________
5. ________________________________
6. ________________________________
7. ________________________________
8. ________________________________

 ISBN 978-81-8477-747-5

9 this, that, these, those

A Complete the sentences with **this** or **that**.

1. __________ is my new school, Mum.
2. Pupils have to come in through __________ gate.
3. Visitors have to use __________ gate over there.
4. Mum, __________ is my teacher, Mrs Wang.
5. Mrs Wang, __________ is my mother.
6. __________ is May's teacher standing near the flagpole.
7. Mum, __________ is my new friend, Kate.
8. __________ is Mary, my other new friend.
9. __________ is Jack standing by the tree.
10. The bookshop is in __________ building over there.

> **Did You Know**
>
> **This** and **that** are pointing words. You use them to show which one you mean. You use **this** to point to something near you. You use **that** to point to something away from you.

 ISBN 978-81-8477-747-5

B Fill in the blanks with **this, that, these** or **those**. The first one is done for you.

Did You Know

You use **this** and **that** to point to singular nouns.

You use **these** and **those** to point to plural nouns.

1. ___This___ is a violin but ___that___ is a trumpet.

2. __________ are farm animals but __________ is a wild animal.

3. __________ are kingfishers but __________ are pelicans.

4. __________ is my brother and __________ are my friends over there.

 ISBN 978-81-8477-747-5

5. __________ are cricket balls but __________ is a basketball.

6. __________ is my favourite place to eat but __________ is not a very good place to eat.

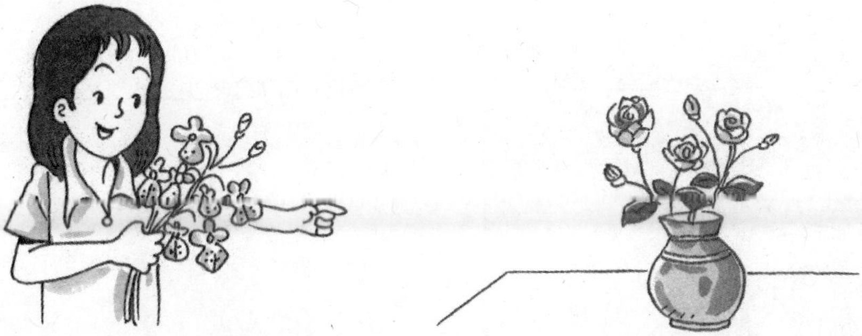

7. __________ are orchids and __________ are roses.

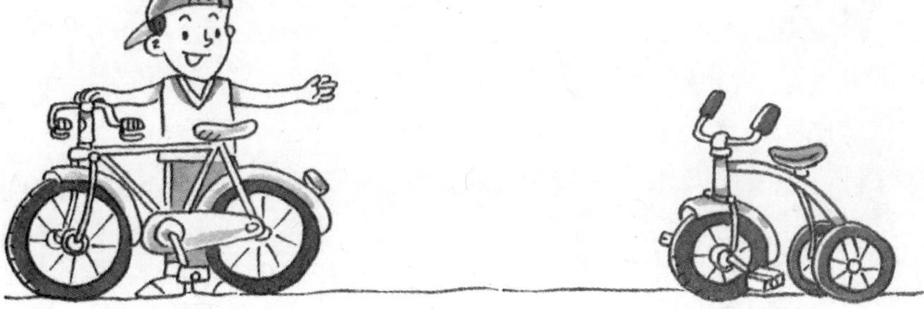

8. __________ is a bicycle but __________ is a tricycle.

 ISBN 978-81-8477-747-5

C Fill in the blanks with **this or that.**

Did You Know

This and **that** can be used to show which person or thing you are pointing to.

1. Stop __________ man.

2. Let's move __________ chair to __________ corner.

3. Bring me __________ ball.

4. __________ hat is too large for me.

5. __________ counter is closed. Please go to __________ one.

 ISBN 978-81-8477-747-5

D *Complete the sentences with **these** or **those**.*

Did You Know?

These is the plural form of **this**.
Those is the plural form of **that**.

1. What are __________ people watching?

2. I don't like __________ small apples.

   Give me __________ large ones.

3. __________ taxis are waiting for passengers.

4. __________ coaches are waiting for tour groups.

5. How much did you pay for __________ books?

 ISBN 978-81-8477-747-5

10 Adjectives

A *Here is part of a story. Read it and underline all the adjectives that describe the nouns in the story.*

When Jack woke up, it was still dark outside. He looked out of the small window and saw that an enormous beanstalk had grown up in the night. He ran outside, and saw that the beanstalk had grown so high that it disappeared into the white clouds. He decided to climb it and eventually reached the top of the clouds.

Jack found, to his amazement, that at the top of the beanstalk was a big castle. He knocked at the huge door of the castle, and it was opened by a large woman. Jack told her that he was tired and hungry after his long journey and asked her for some food. She gave him some bread and cheese and told him he must leave quickly because her husband was a cruel giant who would probably kill him when he came back from hunting. But just at that moment there was a terrible noise. The giant was returning home. Jack ran to a wooden cupboard and hid in it. In came the giant roaring, "Fee fi fo fum, I smell the blood of a man!"

 ISBN 978-81-8477-747-5

Did You Know

Adjectives make stories more interesting to read. **Adjectives** are words that describe nouns.

B ***Write the adjectives you have underlined in the left column. Then write the nouns they describe in the right column.***

Adjectives	Nouns

 ISBN 978-81-8477-747-5

C Some nouns can be made into adjectives by adding -y or -ful. Add -y or -ful to make these words into adjectives.

1. greed __________
2. success __________
3. noise __________
4. help __________
5. power __________
6. dirt __________
7. smoke __________
8. wind __________

Did You Know?

When you add **-y**, to a word ending in **e** you drop the **e** before adding the **y**.

D Choose suitable adjectives you have just made to describe these pictures.

1. a ____________________ face

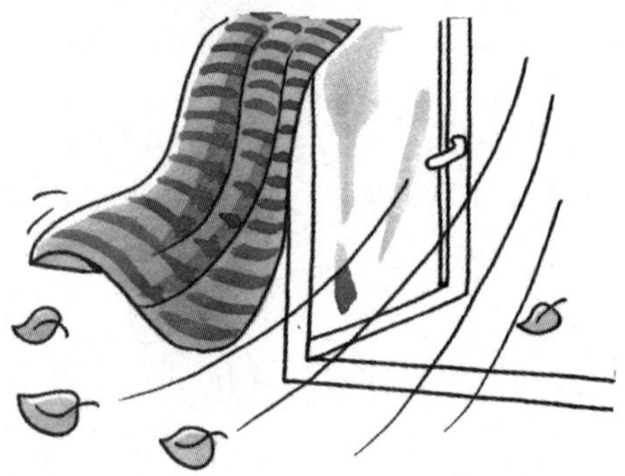

2. a ____________________ day

3. a ____________________ monkey

4. a ____________________ place

E *Some nouns can be made into adjectives by adding **-ful** or **-less**. Add **-ful** or **-less** to make these words into adjectives.*

1. sorrow ____________
2. beauty ____________
3. tooth ____________
4. home ____________
5. sleeve ____________
6. pain ____________
7. cord ____________
8. cheer ____________

Did You Know?

The ending **-ful** means **full of**.

The ending **-less** means **without**.

F *Choose suitable adjectives you have just made to describe these pictures.*

1. ________________________ children

2. a ________________________ T-shirt

3. a ________________________ phone

4. a ________________________ lady

 ISBN 978-81-8477-747-5

11 More about Adjectives

A *Read the story and look at the two words in bold.* ***Kinder*** *is called a* ***comparative adjective*** *and* ***kindest*** *is called a* ***superlative adjective.*** *Find five other adjectives that compare in the story and underline them.*

Mei Min was a very kind little girl. She was **kinder** than her sister. She was kinder than her brother. In fact, she was the **kindest** person in her family.

One day Mei Min met three big homeless dogs. She patted the white one. He was big. She patted the brown one. He was even bigger, but the biggest of all was the black one and he looked very hungry.

 ISBN 978-81-8477-747-5

"Come with me," she invited the dogs. "I will find you something to eat." She knew her mother had just baked some pastries which were on the highest kitchen shelf. Mei Min climbed on to a chair and gave the dogs a pastry each.

When her sister saw the empty pie plate, she was angry. Her father was even angrier, and her mother was the angriest of all. "I'm sorry," said Mei Min. "But I only gave the dogs my share of the pastries. I don't mind not having any."

Her brother and sister both said, "The dogs can have my share too."

"OK," said her father. "Let's buy some dog food and then we will share the rest of the pastries." Mei Min smiled. She was sure that the dogs were smiling also.

B *Use the correct adjectives to complete this exercise.*

Did You Know

You can use **adjectives** to compare two or more people, things or feelings.

1. The white dog is big.

   ______________________ is bigger.

   ______________________ is the biggest.

2. Mei Min's sister was angry.

   ______________________ was angrier.

   ______________________ was the angriest.

3. The pastries were on which shelf?

   ____

   ____

 ISBN 978-81-8477-747-5

C Draw a line to join the pair of adjectives that mean the same.

1. beautiful •	• small
2. little •	• chilly
3. untidy •	• lovely
4. cold •	• glittery
5. sparkling •	• messy

D Add a suitable noun to each adjective.

1. a beautiful ____________
2. a lovely ____________
3. a little ____________
4. a small ____________
5. an untidy ____________
6. a messy ____________
7. a cold ____________
8. a chilly ____________
9. a sparkling ____________
10. a glittery ____________

E Draw a line to join the pair of adjectives that are opposite.

1. difficult •	• last
2. dry •	• wet
3. empty •	• old
4. first •	• easy
5. new •	• wide
6. narrow •	• full

 ISBN 978-81-8477-747-5

F Fill in the blanks with suitable adjectives from the box.

1. as ________________ as a fox
2. as ________________ as ABC
3. as ________________ as a tortoise
4. as ________________ as a feather
5. as ________________ as a mouse
6. as ________________ as honey
7. as ________________ as a needle
8. as ________________ as a bull
9. as ________________ as a bee
10. as ________________ as ice

sharp
slow
easy
cold
busy
quiet
strong
sly
light
sweet

 ISBN 978-81-8477-747-5

12 Adverbs

A *Read this story and take note of the words in bold. Then put a ✔ against the correct answer for the following questions.*

Miss Wang was unhappy because the pupils in her class were doing **badly.** They came into the classroom **noisily.** Alice did her maths **slowly** and very **untidily.** Patrick worked **quickly** but he made a lot of mistakes. Tom's work was **poorly** set out and he had ruled his page very **carelessly.**

Miss Wang spoke **quietly** but **firmly** to the class. "Please listen **carefully** to me. It is not so important that you work **quickly.** It is more important that you work **neatly** and **correctly**, and that you write **clearly.**"

"We promise to try much harder," said the students **politely** because they liked Miss Wang.

1. What is special about the words in bold?

   These words tell us more about
   - ☐ people.
   - ☐ things.
   - ☐ actions.

2. What do you call these words?
   - ☐ adjectives
   - ☐ adverbs
   - ☐ pronouns

> *Show your teacher you can do these actions:*
> - Laugh **loudly**
> - Smile **happily**
> - Limp **painfully**
> - Frown **fiercely**

 ISBN 978-81-8477-747-5

B ***Choose the best adverb from the box to complete the sentence that will match each picture.***

safely	greedily	slowly
quickly	noisily	bravely

Did You Know

Many adverbs end in **-ly**.

1. The magic beans grew

_____________ .

2. The soldiers fought

_____________ .

3. The monkeys chattered

_____________ .

4. The old lady walked

_____________ .

5. The plane landed _____________ .

6. The fat man ate _____________ .

 ISBN 978-81-8477-747-5

C ***Change the adjective at the top of each picture into adverb. Then write a sentence about the picture using the adverb.***

1. bright — brightly

The sun shone brightly.

____

2. heavy — _______

____

____

3. strong — _______

____

____

4. gentle — _______

____

____

5. soft — _______

____

____

6. smart — _______

____

____

 ISBN 978-81-8477-747-5

D Fill in the blanks with suitable adverbs from the box.

quietly	**clumsily**	**honestly**	**happily**
carefully	**loudly**	**gracefully**	**fortunately**

1. You must answer the policeman ____________ .
2. He is driving ____________ because it is raining.

3. The prince and princess

   lived ____________ ever after.

4. She skated ____________ .
5. Eat your soup ____________ .
6. A hippo moves ____________ .

7. The phone rang ____________ .
8. The car crashed into a tree

   but ____________ the driver was not hurt.

 ISBN 978-81-8477-747-5

13 Prepositions

A ***Read this story and fill in the blanks with the correct prepositions. You will have to use some prepositions more than once.***

at, about, for, from, of, into, above

The Fox and the Grapes

Fox was hungry. At noon, he went out __________ a walk and saw some grapes hanging down __________ a high vine. He started to jump as high as he could __________ the air, snapping __________ the grapes __________ him, but still he could not reach them. After trying __________ a long, long time, Fox gave up and, looking up __________ the grapes, he said, "Well, I don't care __________ those grapes. They are probably sour anyway."

This is how the saying "sour grapes" started. Whenever you hear somebody criticizing something that you know they have no chance __________ getting, you can say it is a case __________ sour grapes.

 ISBN 978-81-8477-747-5

B Fill in the blanks with the correct prepositions.

between	**in**	**over**
across	**under**	**inside**

Did You Know?

A **preposition** usually has a noun or pronoun **after** it.

1. The parachutist landed ________ the circle.

2. There is a boat ________ the bridge.

3. The goalkeeper is standing ________ the poles.

4. They are staying ________ the house because of the rain.

5. There are a lot of buildings ________ the river.

6. The dog jumped ________ the fence.

 ISBN 978-81-8477-747-5

C ***Where are Tom's things? Compare the two pictures and complete the sentences on page 53 using suitable prepositions of position.***

behind in on over under next to

 ISBN 978-81-8477-747-5

Where should Tom's things be?

1. His pillow should be ______________________________

   ____.

2. His books should be ______________________________

   ____.

3. His chair should be ______________________________

   ____.

4. His towel should be hanging ______________________

   ____.

5. The lamp should be standing ______________________

   ____.

6. His pencils should be ____________________________

   ____.

7. The clock should be ______________________________

   ____.

8. His school bag should be hanging _________________

   ____.

 ISBN 978-81-8477-747-5

D ***Prepositions can tell us about time. Fill in the blanks with suitable prepositions of time from the box. Some of them will be used in more than one sentence.***

at	on	before	after	in

Did You Know

Prepositions are small words that help to link nouns and pronouns to other words in a sentence.

1. Dad finishes work __________ half past five.
2. We reach school __________ 7.00 a.m. every day.
3. All the shops close __________ New Year's Day.
4. It's hot __________ the afternoon.
5. Uncle Simon was born __________ 1938.
6. Most animals hunt __________ the day and sleep __________ night.
7. There is a public holiday __________ Wednesday.
8. Trains stop running __________ midnight.
9. I will drive you home __________ school.
10. We will take a shower __________ our swimming practice.

 ISBN 978-81-8477-747-5

14 Verbs *be*

A *Compare the two pictures. Write sentences to show what is different in picture B. Use* ***is, are, isn't*** *or* ***aren't*** *in your sentences. The first one has been done for you.*

n Picture B ...

1. There **aren't** any flowers on the table.
2. ______________________
3. ______________________
4. ______________________
5. ______________________

Did You Know

The words **is** and **are** are verbs **be**.
You use **is** or **isn't** with singular nouns.
You use **are** or **aren't** with plural nouns.

 ISBN 978-81-8477-747-5

B ***Re-write the sentences using short forms for the words in bold print. Look at the pictures and circle true or false.***

1. The bottle **is not** full.

____

____

true *false*

2. This vase **is not** for sale.

____

____

true *false*

3. These children **are not** friends.

____

____

true *false*

4. They **are not** eating their dinner.

____

____

true *false*

 ISBN 978-81-8477-747-5

C ***Read this information about dinosaurs. Underline the words from the verb be.***

Tyrannosaurus Rex was a meat-eater that ate other dinosaurs. Its head was as long as a man's body. It was the king of all the reptiles. The T-Rex was the biggest meat-eating animal that ever lived. It was also the last dinosaur on earth.

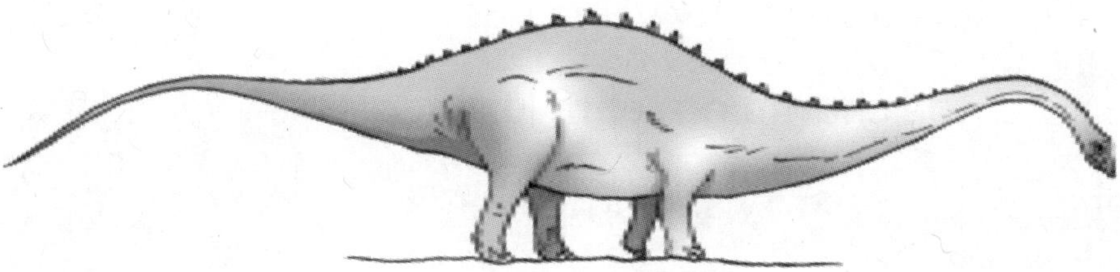

The Diplodocus was one of the longest dinosaurs. It was not very heavy for its size. Diplodocuses were about 30 to 45 metres long. Diplodocuses were plant-eaters and they lived in groups.

The Ornitholestes was a small dinosaur. It was about 2 metres long. Ornitholestes were good hunters in thick forests. They were meat-eaters but also ate things that other dinosaurs killed.

Did You Know?

Was is the past tense of **is** and **am**.
Were is the past tense of **are**.
All these are words from the verb **be**.

 ISBN 978-81-8477-747-5

D *Fill in the blanks with **was** or **were**.*

1. They ________ neighbours before the family moved to Jurong.
2. He ________ a good runner when he was younger.

3. Mr Krishnan ________ a soldier during the war.
4. It ________ a busy morning for me yesterday.
5. She ________ a nurse many years ago.

6. We ________ the champion team last year.
7. My sister ________ sorry she had been naughty last week.

8. Dinosaurs ________ huge animals that lived long ago.
9. You ________ late again yesterday.
10. I ________ in Grade 2 last year.

E *Complete these rules.*

1. You use **was** with the pronouns ________, ________, ________, ________.
2. You use **were** with the pronouns ________, ________, ________.
3. You use **was** with ________________ (singular/plural) nouns.
4. You use **were** with ________________ (singular/plural) nouns.

 ISBN 978-81-8477-747-5

15 Questions

A *Read the questions. Look at the pictures and use the given words to answer the questions. The first one has been done for you.*

1\. Is Mark well?

is / isn't

Yes, he is. ________ No, he isn't. ________

2\. Is it sunny?

is / isn't

________ ________

3\. Are these apples?

are / aren't

________ ________

4\. Are they happy?

are / aren't

________ ________

5\. Is the dog friendly?

is / isn't

________ ________

 ISBN 978-81-8477-747-5

B *Answer these questions.*
Use the words from the box in your answers.

am	is	are	was	were	am not
isn't	aren't	wasn't	weren't		

1. Is it your birthday next week?

2. Are you seven years old?

3. Is your hair black?

4. Are your eyes blue?

5. Is your teacher tall?

6. Were all the students in your class present yesterday?

7. Were you present yesterday?

8. Was your teacher happy with your work last week?

 ISBN 978-81-8477-747-5

C *When Mrs Wang came back from shopping, this was the mess she saw. What questions would she ask her children? Use **how, what, where, when, why, who, which** in your questions.*

Remember
You need to put a question mark at the end of each question.

1. How ______________________________

____

2. What ______________________________

____

3. Where ______________________________

____

4. When ______________________________

____

5. Why ______________________________

____

6. Who ______________________________

____

7. Which ______________________________

____

 ISBN 978-81-8477-747-5

D ***Write the name of someone you know on the first line. Use the given words to ask this person about his or her life.***

____

1. Where ______________________________
____
______________________________?

2. When ______________________________
____
______________________________?

3. Why ______________________________
____
______________________________?

4. Who ______________________________
____
______________________________?

5. What ______________________________
____
______________________________?

6. How ______________________________
______________________________?

 ISBN 978-81-8477-747-5

16 has, have

A Complete the sentences with **has** or **have**.

1. I __________ a brother and a sister.
2. She __________ a temperature.
3. We __________ a new car.
4. They __________ three children.
5. You __________ a beautiful hat.
6. He __________ a lot of stamps.
7. They __________ no home.
8. Look at that monkey.

   It __________ a long tail.

B Complete these rules.

1. The pronouns that go with **has** are __________, __________, __________.
2. The pronouns that go with **have** are __________, __________,

   __________, __________.

 ISBN 978-81-8477-747-5

C *Choose the correct word from the brackets to complete the sentences.*

1. John ____________ (has, have) mumps.
2. Many people ____________ (has, have) to travel by train.
3. Everyone ____________ (has, have) a ticket.
4. All of us must ____________ (has, have) a good dictionary.
5. These birds ____________ (has, have) very strong beaks.
6. No one ____________ (has, have) full marks for the test.
7. Singapore ____________ (has, have) many interesting places to see.
8. Somebody ____________ (has, have) the key to the door.
9. Mr and Mrs Lee ____________ (has, have) a large family.
10. The house ____________ (has, have) many windows.

D *Complete these rules.*

1. You use **has** with ________________ (singular/plural) nouns.
2. You use **have** with ________________ (singular/plural) nouns.

 ISBN 978-81-8477-747-5

E Write two sentences about these animals and insects. Use **have** or **has** in your sentences.

1. Insects ______________________________

____

____

____

2. Elephants ______________________________

____

____

____

3. A kangaroo ______________________________

____

____

____

4. A tiger ______________________________

____

____

____

5. Cats ______________________________

____

____

____

 ISBN 978-81-8477-747-5

17 do, does, did

A *Read this passage. Underline the verbs **do, does** and **did**. Then circle the **nouns** or **pronouns** in front of the verbs.*

My friend said that his mother does all the work. Their family is lazy. They do some of the work only when his mother asks them.

In my house, we do what we can to help. My father does the shopping. He does it on Saturday. I do the sweeping and my sister does the laundry. She does it with the help of a washing machine. It does the work very quickly. Our family does everything together.

Last night I did my homework and my sister helped me. I did well in last week's test because she helped.

B *Complete these rules.*

1. You use **do** with the pronouns ________, ________, ________, ________.
2. You use **does** with the pronouns ________, ________, ________.
3. You use **do** with ____________ (plural/singular) nouns.
4. You use **does** with ____________ (plural/singular) nouns.
5. **Did** is the ____________ (past/present) tense of **do** and **does.**

 ISBN 978-81-8477-747-5

C Complete the sentences with **do, does** or **did.**

1. I always __________ my homework myself.
2. Mum __________ the cooking.
3. Dad __________ the gardening.
4. The children __________ the washing-up.
5. We __________ what we could to help Mum.
6. Who __________ this drawing?
7. He __________ the painting all by himself last Sunday.
8. She often __________ well in the exams.
9. __________ as you please.
10. The pupils usually __________ their work quickly.

Remember

You use **do** with plural nouns, and the pronouns **I**, **you**, **we** and **they**.

You use **does** with the pronouns **he**, **she** and **it**. You also use **does** with singular nouns.

 ISBN 978-81-8477-747-5

D Re-write the sentences using short forms for the words in bold print. Look at the pictures and circle true or false.

Did You Know?

You can shorten:

does not → doesn't

do not → don't

did not → didn't

1. These shoes **do not** fit me.

   These ______________________________

   ____

   true *false*

2. Dad **does not** go to work on Sunday

   ____

   ____

   true *false*

3. Monkeys **do not** like bananas.

   ____

   ____

   true *false*

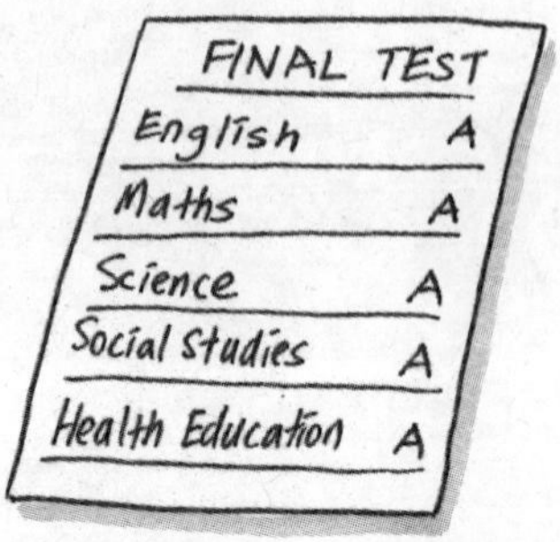

4. This student **did not** do well in his exams.

   ____

   ____

   true *false*

 ISBN 978-81-8477-747-5

18 Tenses

A *Read this story. Circle the verbs with the correct tense.*

Many years ago, in a forest close to town, there (lives / lived) three witches. One of the witches (is / was) kind and friendly, but the other two witches (was / were) mean and unkind.

One day a small girl (wanders / wandered) by the cottage. She (was / were) selling flowers.

"Would you (like / likes) to buy a posy?" she (asks / asked) when the witches (come / came) to the door.

"I (shall / will) buy a posy, if you (come / came) into my cottage," said the first witch.

"I (shall / will) buy a posy, if you (has / have) time to (come / comes) inside," said the second witch.

"They (shall / will) (lock / locks) you up and (make / made) you their servant if you come inside," (warns / warned) the kind witch. "Follow me, I (shall / will) save you."

The little girl (follows / followed) the kind witch out of the forest and (hurries / hurried) home.

 ISBN 978-81-8477-747-5

B ***In each of these sentences there is one verb with a letter missing. Cross it out and re-write the correct verb above it.***

1. It was a wet day and the boy sipped on the path.
2. The hens clucked and the cocks rowed.
3. The holy man payed to God.
4. I will cut up the meat if you cop the vegetables.
5. The boy taked on the phone for hours.
6. The lady witched off the light and went to bed.
7. The dog waked on Dad's new garden.
8. The car topped in our driveway.

 ISBN 978-81-8477-747-5

C *Write in the missing verbs, using the correct tense.*

1. I think Ali will win today.

   He ________________ this race last year.

2. How many times must I tell you?

   I ________________ you the same thing last night.

3. That dog may bite you. He ________________ the postman yesterday.

4. I hope the wind doesn't blow too hard this

   winter. Last winter it ________________ so hard the branches of my tree broke.

5. My brother sits next to Amin in school.

   He ________________ next to him last year too.

6. I felt sorry for you the first time, but you've

   done it again. So I don't ________________ sorry for you now.

 ISBN 978-81-8477-747-5

D What do you think will happen next? Use shall or will in your answers.

> **Did You Know**
>
> You can use **shall** or **will** with **I** and **we.**
>
> You use **will** with **she, he, it, you** and **they.**

1. You ______________________

____

____

2. She ______________________

____

3. They ______________________

____

4. We ______________________

____

5. He ______________________

____

6. It ______________________

____

 ISBN 978-81-8477-747-5

19 Making Sentences

A Join the sentence parts that match.

Who or what?	What action?	Where? How? When? Why?
1. The team	walk	softly.
2. The cat	shone	easily by four goals.
3. Lions	won	very slowly.
4. Old people	cried	brightly.
5. The city lights	purred	when they realized they were lost.
6. The happy girl	roar	at this station.
7. The children	stop	when she saw the clown.
8. All the trains	laughed	loudly.

Re-write the sentences in the spaces below.

1. ______________________________
2. ______________________________
3. ______________________________
4. ______________________________
5. ______________________________
6. ______________________________
7. ______________________________
8. ______________________________

 ISBN 978-81-8477-747-5

B ***Write a sentence to show what each person* is doing *in the picture.***

1. John **is making** a sandcastle.
2. May ______________________________
3. Tom ______________________________
4. Jenny and Melinda ______________________________
5. Mrs Tay ______________________________
6. Mr Tay ______________________________

C ***Now change the sentences you have made into past tense to show what each person* was doing *yesterday.***

1. John **was making** a sandcastle.
2. May ______________________________
3. Tom ______________________________
4. Jenny and Melinda ______________________________
5. Mrs Tay ______________________________
6. Mr Tay ______________________________

 ISBN 978-81-8477-747-5

D ***Ali took this photo in the park last week. Form sentences using the given words to describe what the people were doing in the park.***

riding his bike	feeding the ducks	reading a book
throwing a ball	eating her lunch	listening to the radio
sleeping under a tree	paddling a canoe	

1. One boy was riding his bike.
2. Another boy ______
3. Another boy ______
4. One girl ______
5. Another girl ______
6. A small girl ______
7. A man ______
8. A woman ______

 ISBN 978-81-8477-747-5

20 Connectors

A *Look at the pictures. Form sentences using the word* ***when.***

When I...	**I do this**

1. **When** I feel sad I cry.

2. ______________________________

3. ______________________________

____

Did You Know

Connectors can be called **conjunctions.**

 ISBN 978-81-8477-747-5

B *Look at the pictures. Form sentences using the word **when**.*

What I do ... **when ...**

Did You Know

You can use **when** to join two sentences together.

1. I jump on to a chair **when** I see a mouse.

2. ______________________________

____

3. ______________________________

____

 ISBN 978-81-8477-747-5

C *This is what May did while she waited for Mum.*
Write sentences that tell what she did using the word ***while.***

1. May drew a picture **while** she waited for Mum.
2. May ______________________________
____
3. May ______________________________
____

Did You Know

You can use **while** and **as** to join two sentences together.

D *Look at the pictures. They show what happened just as Jade walked to the door. Form sentences using the word* ***as.***

1. **As** Jade walked through the door, the cat ran out.
2. ______________________________
____
____
3. ______________________________
____
____

 ISBN 978-81-8477-747-5

E ***The pictures show what Jean did before she went to school. Write sentences about what she did using the word before.***

1. Jean brushed her teeth **before** she went to school.

2. Jean ______________________________

____

3. Jean ______________________________

____

4. Jean ______________________________

____

 ISBN 978-81-8477-747-5

This is what Salim did after he arrived home from school. Write sentences that tell what he did using the word after.

5. Salim read a book **after** he arrived home from school.

6. Salim ______________________________

____

7. Salim ______________________________

____

8. Salim ______________________________

____

____

Did You Know?

You can use **before** and **after** to join two sentences together.

 ISBN 978-81-8477-747-5

F Read the passage and write sentences using the word since.

Tom and Lisa live in Singapore. Their Grandma lives in America. She visits them every Christmas. Look at the pictures. What has changed **since** Grandma's last visit?

Last year **This year**

1. Tom has grown taller **since** Grandma last visited.

2. ______________________________

____

3. ______________________________

____

 ISBN 978-81-8477-747-5

Page 6

A This clown can juggle twenty-six balls.

Page 7

B 1. bucket 2. pizza 3. jeep
4. sail 5. school 6. mail
7. beak 8. cube 9. cake
10. beans

C Answers may vary.

Page 8

D 1. Dora 2. Eric 3. Fuad
4. Grace 5. John 6. Kate
7. May 8. Richard 9. Siti
10. Zena
1. Animals in Danger
2. Cooking for Kids 3. Dinosaurs
4. Kites 5. Lions 6. Planets
7. Soccer Champions 8. Trains

Page 9

E Answers may vary.

Page 10

A 1. an eel. 2. an apple.
3. a belt. 4. a fish. 5. a scarf.

Page 11

B 1. a 2. a 3. an 4. the
5. The 6. An 7. the 8. the
9. a 10. an

C a... young kitten; very good choice
an... old man; active kitten
the... orange kitten; black one; cage
1. an 2. a

Page 12

D 1. An, an 2. A, a, a 3. the
4. an 5. a, the 6. the, a
7. an, a, a, the 8. an, the
9. The, the 10. the, the, the

E *A* is used in the first sentence because the word 'river' begins with a consonant.
The is used in the second sentence because 'Amazon River' is a special name for a river.

Page 13

F Jack was sitting in a park looking very unhappy. There were not many people in the park. An old man sat down next to him and asked Jack why he was so sad.

"I want to see a movie, but I don't have any money. My mum says that she doesn't have very much money to spare."

"When I was young," said the old man, "we didn't have much money either. We had few treats. My friends made some
money by washing cars, so that we could all go to the movies together. I guess very few people share what they have these days."

"Maybe I could ask some neighbours if I could help them wash their cars. Then I might have enough money to take someone to the movies with me. Would you like to come?" asked Jack.

G 2. money, neighbours 3. people
4. money 5. money

Page 14

A 1. goat 2. ostrich
3. monkey 4. lion
5. orang utan

B 1. chick 2. kitten 3. calf
4. tadpole

Page 15

A 6. hippo 7. crocodile
8. sea lion 9. polar bear
10. penguin

B 5. puppy 6. foal 7. duckling
8. kid

Page 16

C **People:** dentist; clown; king; artist
Animals: calf; cat; frog; ape
Places: school; playground; airport; castle
Things: soap; pan; car; net

D 1. eyes 2. hands 3. nose
4. ears 5. mouth 6. tongue
7. teeth 8. head

Page 17

1 d													
e		2 z			3 p								
4 e	l	e	p	h	a	n	5 t						
r		b			n		i						
		r			d		6 g	i	r	a	f	f	e
		a			7 a	p	e						
							8 r	h	i	n	o		

Page 18

A Mammals are a special group of animals that do not lay eggs. They have live babies and feed their young on milk.

Mammals have fur on their bodies. Some of them have really thick fur.

Most mammals live on land, but some, like the dolphins and whales, live in the sea. Mice and rats build nests in dark places, while squirrels make their homes in hollow trees.

All mammals breathe air through their lungs, so mammals that live in water have to come to the top to breathe or they will drown.

Some mammals you may know are:
dogs and cats
goats and donkeys
cows and oxen
foxes and wolves

Page 19

B mammals/mammal; dolphins/dolphin; whales/whale; mice/mouse; rats/rat; squirrels/squirrel; dogs /dog; cats/cat; goats/goat; donkeys/donkey; oxen/ox; cows/cow; foxes/fox; wolves/wolf

C 1. girls 2. witches
3. monkeys 4. babies
5. pens 6. boxes
7. ponies 8. boys
9. bananas 10. dishes

Page 20

D 1. children 2. deer
3. geese 4. sheep
5. women 6. fish
7. teeth 8. reindeer

E 1. houses, mice
2. foxes, oxen
3. pans, men
4. boots, feet

Page 21

A **Plural countable nouns:** eggs; vegetables; carrots; tomatoes; beans; peas; apples; oranges; bananas; grapes
Uncountable nouns: salt; cooking oil; sugar; butter; cheese; milk; fish; chicken; meat

Page 22

B 1. sister, cockroaches
2. weather
3. children, fun
4. hands, food
5. traffic, highway
6. pen
7. fire
8. bookshop, books, magazines
9. clouds, sky
10. wind

Countable Nouns: sister, cockroaches, children, hands, highway, pen, bookshop, books, magazines, clouds
Uncountable Nouns: weather, fun, food, traffic, fire, sky, wind

Page 23

D 1. a few plates/mugs/glasses/spoons
2. a little sugar/milk/juice
3. plenty of sugar/milk/juice
4. some bread/milk/juice/coffee/sugar/ cheese/butter
5. an egg
6. four spoons/mugs

Page 24

A At Christmas-time, my family and I went to London.

London is a big city in England. When we arrived, the first thing we did was to visit Buckingham Palace. I wish I could take a photo of Queen Elizabeth or Prince Charles.

 ISBN 978-81-8477-747-5

The tour guide and the bus driver both told me that there are many important people in England, like lords and ladies, dukes and duchesses, but they don't all live in palaces.

Tomorrow we are going to the London Zoo.

Page 25

B **Masculine Nouns:** Prince, lords, dukes
Feminine Nouns: Queen, ladies, duchesses
Common-gender Nouns: tour guide, bus driver

Page 26

C 1. uncle — aunt; rooster — hen; stallion — mare; drake — duck; groom — bride; nephew — niece
2. lioness; tigress; cow elephant; vixen; goose; peahen
3. cub — lion/tiger/bear/wolf
calf — bull/elephant/whale/giraffe
pup — dog/fox/seal

Page 27

D **Masculine Nouns:**
1. steward 7. lion
8. Tim 10. duke
Feminine Nouns:
2. maid 4. mum
10. queen
Common-gender Nouns:
1. passengers 3. teachers
4. cousin 5. people
6. children 9. zookeeper

Page 28

A During the school holidays, Maggie and her parents flew to London with Singapore Airlines. They left Singapore on 10 June.

They stayed at the Regency Hotel. They went to the Tower of London, the British Museum and Hyde Park. They also went to the famous Harrods department store to buy some souvenirs for Maggie's friends, Nancy, Doris and Ben. Maggie also bought a photo frame for her Uncle Andy and Aunt Susie.

Maggie enjoyed her holiday.

B **People:** Nancy; Doris; Ben; Uncle Andy; Aunt Susie
Places: Singapore; Regency Hotel; Tower of London; British Museum; Hyde Park; Harrods

Page 29

C 1. Mary, John and David were helping Miss Lee, the librarian, in the school library. Their school is in Chestnut Road.
2. John took four books to the Children's Section. They were Alice in Wonderland, Aesop's Fables, Harry Potter and Gulliver's Travels.
3. Mary took three books to the Reference Section. They were First Learners' Dictionary, English for Children and The World Atlas.
4. David took two books to the History Section. They were A History of the World and Famous Battles.
5. Miss Lee thanked the children for helping.

Page 30

D Answers may vary.

Page 31

E Answers may vary.

Page 32

A Hello, my name is Peter. I live in the city with my mother and father and two sisters. My father is a teacher. He works very long hours. My mother is a lawyer, but she only works part-time. My sisters and I try to help our parents as much as we can. My sisters help in the kitchen. They wash and dry the dishes. I make my own bed and keep my room tidy. I have a cat called Ginger. It has lived with us for a long time.

B **Singular Pronouns:** he, she, it
Plural Pronouns: they, us

Page 33

C 1. It 2. He 3. They
4. I 5. She 6. you
7. We
D 1. me 2. it 3. us
4. them 5. you 6. her
7. him

Page 34

E 1. They 2. I 3. She
4. It/She/He 5. He
6. We 7. You 8. You
F 2. I'm eight years old.
3. She's talking to her friend.
4. It's/He's/She's barking at the stranger.
5. He's made it by himself.
6. We're good friends.
7. You've missed the bus.
8. You've done well!

Page 35

A 1. This 2. this 3. that
4. this 5. this 6. That
7. this 8. This 9. That
10. that

Page 36

B 2. These, that 3. These, those
4. This, those

Page 37

5. These, that 6. This, that
7. These, those 8. This, that

Page 38

C 1. that 2. this, that 3. that
4. This 5. This, that

Page 39

D 1. those 2. these, those
3. These 4. Those 5. these

Page 40

A When Jack woke up, it was still dark outside. He looked out of the small window and saw that an enormous beanstalk had grown up in the night. He ran outside, and saw that the beanstalk had grown so high that it disappeared into the white clouds. He decided to climb it and eventually reached the top of the clouds.

Jack found, to his amazement, that at the top of the beanstalk was a big castle. He knocked at the huge door of the castle, and it was opened by a large woman. Jack told her that he was tired and hungry after his long journey and asked her for some food. She gave him some bread and cheese and told him he must leave quickly because her husband was a cruel giant who would probably kill him when he came back from hunting. But just at that moment there was a terrible noise. The giant was returning home. Jack ran to a wooden cupboard and hid in it. In came the giant roaring, "Fee fi fo fum, I smell the blood of a man!"

Page 41

B

Adjectives	Nouns
small	window
enormous	beanstalk
white	clouds
big	castle
huge	door
large	woman
long	journey
cruel	giant
terrible	noise
wooden	cupboard

Page 42

C 1. greedy 2. successful
3. noisy 4. helpful
5. powerful 6. dirty
7. smoky 8. windy
D 1. dirty 2. windy
3. greedy 4. noisy

Page 43

E 1. sorrowful 2. beautiful
3. toothless 4. homeless
5. sleeveless
6. painful/painless
7. cordless 8. cheerful

 ISBN 978-81-8477-747-5

F 1. cheerful 2. sleeveless
3. cordless 4. beautiful

Page 44

A Mei Min was a very kind little girl. She was kinder than her sister. She was kinder than her brother. In fact, she was the kindest person in her family.

One day Mei Min met three big homeless dogs. She patted the white one. He was big. She patted the brown one. He was even bigger, but the biggest of all was the black one and he looked very hungry.

"Come with me," she invited the dogs.
"I will find you something to eat." She knew her mother had just baked some pastries which were on the highest kitchen shelf. Mei Min climbed on to a chair and gave the dogs a pastry each.

Page 45

When her sister saw the empty pie plate, she was angry. Her father was even angrier, and her mother was the angriest of all. "I'm sorry," said Mei Min. "But I only gave the dogs my share of the pastries. I don't mind not having any."

Her brother and sister both said, "The dogs can have my share too."

"OK," said her father. "Let's buy some dog food and then we will share the rest of the pastries."

Mei Min smiled. She was sure that the dogs were smiling also.

B 1. The brown dog is bigger.
The black dog is the biggest.
2. Her father was angrier.
Her mother was the angriest.
3. On the highest shelf.

Page 46

C 1. beautiful - lovely
2. little - small
3. untidy - messy
4. cold - chilly
5. sparkling - glittery

D Answers may vary.

E 1. difficult - easy 2. dry - wet
3. empty - full 4. first - last
5. new - old
6. narrow - wide

Page 47

F 1. sly 2. easy 3. slow
4. lazy 5. quiet 6. sweet
7. sharp 8. strong 9. busy
10. cold

Page 48

A 1. actions 2. adverbs

Page 49

B 1. quickly 2. bravely 3. noisily
4. slowly 5. safely
6. greedily

Page 50

D 2. heavily 3. strongly 4. gently
5. softly 6. smartly

Page 51

D 1. honestly 2. carefully
3. happily 4. gracefully
5. quietly 6. clumsily
7. loudly 8. fortunately

Page 52

A Fox was hungry. At noon, he went out for a walk and saw some grapes hanging down from a high vine. He started to jump as high as he could into the air, snapping at the grapes above him, but still he could not reach them. After trying for a long time, Fox gave up and, looking up at the grapes, he said, "Well, I don't care about those grapes. They are probably sour anyway."

This is how the saying "sour grapes" started. Whenever you hear somebody criticizing something that you know they have no chance of getting, you can say it is a case of sour grapes.

Page 53

B 1. in 2. under
3. between 4. inside
5. across 6. over

Page 55

1. His pillow should be on the bed.
2. His books should be in the bookcase/ on the book shelves.
3. His chair should be under the desk.
4. His towel should be hanging over the towel rack.
5. The lamp should be standing next to the bed.
6. His pencils should be in the pencil holder/jar.
7. The clock should be on the bedside table.
8. His school bag should be hanging behind the door.

Page 56

D 1. at/before 2. at/before
3. on 4. in
5. in 6. in, at
7. on 8. at
9. after 10. after

Page 57

A There isn't a bottle of sauce/ ketchup.
There are two candles.
There are six glasses.
There is a jug.

Page 58

B 1. isn't — true 2. isn't — false
3. aren't — false
4. aren't — true

Page 59

C Tyrannosaurus Rex was a meat-eater that ate other dinosaurs. Its head was as long as a man's body. It was the king of all the reptiles. The T-Rex was the biggest meat-eating animal that ever lived. It was also the last dinosaur on earth.

The Diplodocus was one of the longest dinosaurs. It was not very heavy for its size. Diplodocuses were about 30 to 45 metres long. Diplodocuses were plant-eaters and they lived in groups.

The Ornitholestes was a small dinosaur. It was about 2 metres long. Ornitholestes were good hunters in thick forests. They were meat-eaters but also ate things that other dinosaurs killed.

Page 60

D 1. were 2. was 3. was
4. was 5. was 6. were
7. was 8. were 9. were
10. was

E 1. I, he, she, it
2. you, we, they
3. singular
4. plural

Page 61

A 2. No, it isn't. Yes, it is.
3. Yes, they are. No, they aren't.
4. No, they aren't. Yes, they are.
5. No, it isn't. Yes, it is.

Page 62

B 1. Yes, it is. / No, it isn't.
2. Yes, I am. / No, I am not.
3. Yes, it is. / No, it isn't.
4. Yes, they are. / No, they aren't.
5. Yes, she is. / Yes, he is. / No, she isn't./No, he isn't.
6. Yes, they were. / No, they weren't.
7. Yes, I was. / No, I wasn't.
8. Yes, she was. / Yes, he was. / No, she wasn't. / No, he wasn't.

Page 63

C Answers may vary.

Page 64

D Answers may vary.

Page 65

A 1. have 2. has 3. have
4. have 5. have 6. has
7. have 8. has

B 1. she, he, it
2. I, you, we, they

Page 66

C 1. has 2. have 3. has

 ISBN 978-81-8477-747-5

4. have 5. have 6. has
7. has 8. has 9. have
10. has

D 1. singular 2. plural

Page 67

E Answers may vary.

Page 68

A My friend said that his mother does all the work. Their family is lazy. They do some of the work only when his mother asked them.

In my house, we do what we can to help. My father does the shopping. He does it on Saturday. I do the sweeping and my sister does the laundry. She does it with the help of a washing machine. It does the work very quickly. Our family does everything together.

Last night I did my homework and my sister helped me. I did well in last week's test because she helped.

B 1. I, you, we, they 2. she, he, it
3. plural 4. singular 5. past

Page 69

C 1. do 2. does 3. does
4. do 5. did 6. did
7. did 8. does 9. Do
10. do

Page 70

D 1. don't — true 2. doesn't — true
3. don't — false 4. didn't — false

Page 71

A lived; was; were; wandered; was; like; asked; came; shall; come; shall; have; come; will; lock; make; warned; shall; followed; hurried

Page 72

B 1. slipped 2. crowed
3. prayed 4. chop
5. talked 6. switched
7. walked 8. stopped

Page 73

C 1. won 2. told 3. bit
4. blew 5. sat 6. feel

Page 74

D Answers may vary.

Page 75

A 2. The cat purred softly.
3. Lions roar loudly.
4. Old people walk very slowly.
5. The city lights shone brightly.
6. The happy girl laughed when she saw the clown.
7. The children cried when they realized they were lost.
8. All the trains stop at this station.

Page 76

B Answers may vary.

C Answers may vary.

Page 77

D 2. Another boy was reading a book.
3. Another boy was listening to the radio.
4. One girl was feeding the ducks.
5. Another girl was paddling a canoe.
6. A small girl was throwing a ball.
7. A man was sleeping under a tree.
8. A woman was eating her lunch.

Page 78

A Answers may vary.

Page 79

B Answers may vary.

Page 80

C Answers may vary.

D Answers may vary.

Page 81

E Answers may vary.

Page 82

Answers may vary.

Page 83

F Answers may vary.

 ISBN 978-81-8477-747-5